THE HAUNTED SURFBOARD

Anthony Masters

Illustrated by Peter Dennis

A & C Black • London

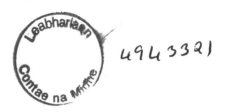

THE HAUNTED SURFBOARD

No.

This edition published 2008
First published 1999 by
A & C Black Publishers Ltd
38 Soho Square, London, W1D 3HB

www.acblack.com

ISBN 978-0-7136-8639-5

A CIP catalogue for this book is available
from the British Library.

This book is produced using paper that is made from wood
grown in managed, sustainable forests. It is natural, renewable and
recyclable. The logging and manufacturing processes conform to
the environmental regulations of the country of origin.

Printed and bound in China by C&C Offset Printing Co.,Ltd.

CHAPTER ONE

Jack Morton raced after his classmate, yelling furiously.

Jack didn't really want to get into a fight, but there didn't seem much alternative. Darren had grabbed his lunch box and was refusing to give it back.

Jack threw himself at Darren, knocking the lunch box to the ground. As the two boys fought, they lost their balance, and were soon rolling around on the floor.

Mr Dawkins, their teacher, was there in seconds.

As Darren went off with his mates, Mr Dawkins took Jack aside.

You're not making friends very easily, are you?

Mr Dawkins smiled. He didn't want to be too hard on Jack. He knew that Jack's parents had recently split up and that he and his mother had moved to Cornwall to make a fresh start.

No one likes me here.

But I don't care. Everyone in Cornwall is soft. I used to be a hard guy in London.

Jack picked up his lunch box and walked slowly away.
He missed his dad and he missed London. Why had
Mum dragged him down to this dump?

At least the dump had waves.

That evening Jack forgot all about his problems at school as he paddled out to sea on his surfboard.

There was no one else around and Jack was disappointed. He did want to make friends. Even if the other kids at school wouldn't accept him, surely the surfers would. But the beach was long and lonely and, as usual, deserted.

Jack sat on his board staring out to sea. As he waited for a good wave, he thought about his fight with Darren.

Will I ever make friends?

Then he saw the wave rolling up.

Excited, he waited for the right moment to make his move.

With expert timing, Jack caught the roller and stood up on his board. He rode the crest, his heart thumping with excitement as the wave carried him in.

As Jack turned to paddle back out, he noticed a boy surfing near the rocks.

Oi!

You aren't allowed over there. Haven't you seen the warning signs?

The thundering of the surf was too loud for the boy to hear.

Jack was puzzled. Where had the boy come from? He glanced back at the summer cottages at the head of the beach. It was early May and his was the only one rented out.

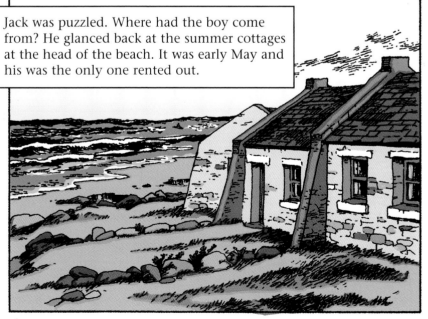

Then he saw his mother walking down the beach towards him.

Time for dinner.

That boy — he's in trouble.

What boy?

Out by the rocks.

His mother gazed out to sea.

I don't see anyone.

The rock was partly submerged and clouded with spray, but Jack could see that it was covered with razor-sharp barnacles.

Then the boy disappeared.

Call for help!

Where are you going?

He needs help. I've got to get out there!

Then you'll both be in trouble. Stay here, Jack. You must stay here!

15

CHAPTER TWO

Jack approached the rocks carefully, trying not to be pulled towards them by the current and the pounding waves.

But when he got closer, Jack could see no sign of the boy at all. He seemed to have vanished without a trace.

Where are you?

I'm here to help.

Suddenly, Jack saw a ledge above him. He grabbed at a mass of seaweed, kicked away his board, and managed to pull himself up.

Where are you?

I've come to help. Now you'll have to help me.

Then with relief, Jack saw someone swimming towards him. Through the spray, he saw a jeep on the beach. It was a lifeguard, responding to his mother's emergency call.

19

Of course not. It must have been a trick of the light or something.

You know this beach isn't lifeguard patrolled, don't you?

Yes.

Don't try this stunt again, whatever you do. Just call us. I'm going to put you on a line, OK? The tide's going out and the surf won't be so high.

Jack hesitated.

What's the matter?

Any chance of getting my board back?

The lifeguard glanced to the right and Jack followed his gaze. His board was rammed into a crack in the rock and had broken in two.

Once the lifeguard had got him back to the beach and delivered another safety lecture, he drove off. Mrs Morton was angry and humiliated.

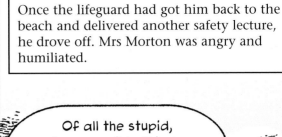

Of all the stupid, irresponsible things to do. You could have drowned out there.

I saw this boy.

No one else did.

CHAPTER THREE

The next evening...

If only I had a board. I'll never save up enough money to buy one this summer.

Jack sat down and gazed out to sea. He felt desperately sorry for himself. Dad had given him the board just before he left home and it was very precious to him.

Suddenly, something in the water caught his eye. It was floating away from the rocks. At first he wasn't sure what it was.

Is it a dead body? No, too flat.

Could it be a surfboard?

Jack watched as it caught the crest of a wave and hurtled towards him, landing in the shallow water.

Jack made a dash for it, pulling the surfboard up the sand. The board was old and battered but beautifully waxed. Jack looked around. There was no one in sight, so he picked it up and headed for home.

His mum was not at all pleased to see the surfboard.

It just floated in towards me.

But it doesn't belong to you!

Jack knew that she didn't want him to go back into the sea.

Look, Mum, if anyone claims this board, I'll give it back to them. I promise.

Mrs Morton gazed at her son doubtfully.

The next day was Sunday, and the light and the surf were perfect.

A boy was surfing dangerously near the rocks and he had long, blond hair.

This can't be another trick of the light.

As Jack ran down the beach, however, he wished he had a friend to surf with. Then he came to a sudden halt.

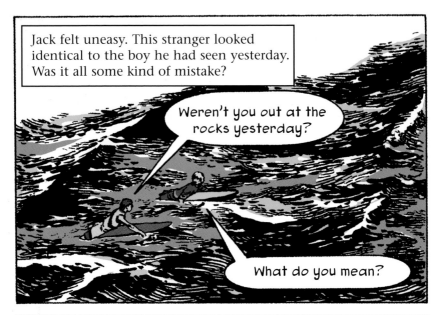

Jack felt uneasy. This stranger looked identical to the boy he had seen yesterday. Was it all some kind of mistake?

Weren't you out at the rocks yesterday?

What do you mean?

You were surfing near Crab Rock. Too close. I paddled out to warn you, but you disappeared.

It wasn't me.

The boy watched as Jack dragged the board on to the beach.

That belongs to my brother.

Belonged to him, I mean.

I told you, I found it on the beach.

Jack decided not to tell him that the board had floated in from the direction of the rocks.

Jack gasped. Drowned? But he had seen him yesterday. Jack didn't know what to say. Eventually the boy broke the silence.

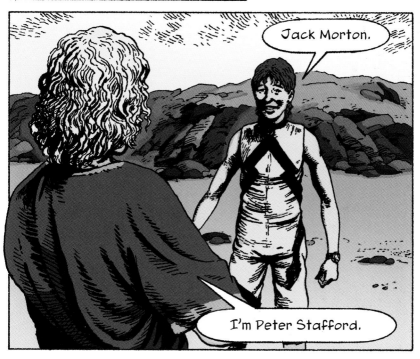

Peter shrugged. There seemed to be nothing to say.

Peter was silent.

Come on. There must be a reason.

You'll laugh.

No, I won't. I promise I won't.

No one else knows this, but I'm trying to get Tom's spirit to rest in peace. You've seen him and so have other people.

I'm sure Tom can't rest until he's surfed that rock, but he'll never do it now because he's dead.

So I'm going to do it for him.

They both gazed out at Crab Rock.

That's a risk I'm going to have to take.

When the surf's high enough, I'm going to give it a try.

CHAPTER FOUR

That night, Jack told his mother about Peter.

I've made a friend.

Who is it?

Peter Stafford. He's staying in the cottage next door. His brother drowned here last year.

Before he went to bed that night, Jack opened his bedroom window and watched the surf gleam in the moonlight. He knew that what Peter was planning was very dangerous. He could drown. But Jack was glad to finally have a friend.

Later that night a huge storm hit. Jack's mother came rushing into his room.

I've never seen the surf so high. Do you think we're going to be flooded?

They stood together at Jack's bedroom window, watching the huge waves. The tide was creeping closer and closer to the house. The spray rose as high as the chimney, and the long fingers of water reached right into their garden.

Jack gazed over at the next-door cottage. Peter had left the surfboard just under the kitchen window, but now it was floating down the garden.

As Jack ran out into the surf-swept garden, he saw Peter coming out of his back door.

The board was on a patch of sand. The wave hadn't been strong enough to drag it out, but there was another one coming.

Jack had always been a fast runner. Now he had to be even faster. The next huge wave was surging towards him.

Jack sprinted across the wet sand towards the board, knowing the wave was already breaking. Any second now, the surf would be hurtling towards him.

He managed to grab the edge of the board as the surf hit him. In dismay, Jack felt the wet surface slip out of his hand and the board jerked away, almost as if someone was pulling it.

Jack fought against the undertow, but it was far too strong for him.

Then, suddenly, he was knocked sideways, as if an unseen hand had pushed him out of the way.

Seconds later, he found himself rolling over on wet sand.

Jack struggled to his feet and raced after Peter.

They ran up the beach and just managed to reach the safety of the cottages before the next wave reached the garden.

51

Jack ran back home, knowing that he was in for a telling off. His mum was waiting for him at the door.

The thunder still growled and the lightning cracked, but the tide was going out now and the cottages were safe.

53

Peter's mum told me. About the loss of her son. Does that board have anything to do with this boy who died?

How could it, Mum?

You're not trying to surf Crab Rock, are you? Like Tom tried to do before he drowned?

No. I promise you I'm not.

At least Jack could be honest about that.

CHAPTER FIVE

The next morning, Jack opened the window and was amazed to see the surfboard lying outside.

Peter's voice spoke again in his mind.

"I bet Tom's playing games with us. He was like that. Always teasing."

Jack crept downstairs and cautiously opened the front door. As he grabbed the board it seemed to move in his hands. Maybe Tom was just playing games.

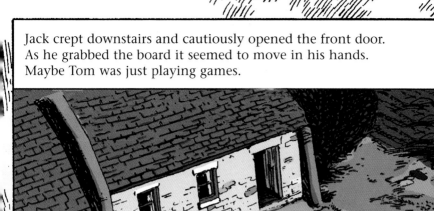

Suddenly, it didn't seem to matter to Jack that the surf wasn't high enough. He forgot about the promise he'd made to his mum.

He turned to Crab Rock and whispered:

For a moment Jack thought he heard a whisper in the wind.

Hoping his mother was still asleep, Jack put on his wetsuit, picked up the surfboard, and ran down the beach towards the surf.

Seconds later, he heard feet pounding on the sand behind him. He turned and saw Peter running towards him.

Suddenly the board flipped over. Its keel almost hit Jack's knee. Peter made a grab for it.

He held on to the board, but again it flipped over. This time it cracked Peter across the shins. He leapt back in pain.

61

The board lay on the sand between them. With a sudden lunge, Peter made another grab for it and then backed off with a sharp cry.

Peter gave a howl of pain as Jack pulled it out.

63

They looked out to sea. The surf was crashing against Crab Rock and the spray was rising up into the early morning sky.

Peter picked up the surfboard and began to walk down to the edge of the water.

CHAPTER SIX

As Peter paddled out into the surf with Jack swimming behind him, the sun came out, turning the waves gold. Peter steered close to Crab Rock, and waited for a wave of the right height.

67

Peter was about to reply when he saw a huge wave in the distance. Jack saw it, too. If Peter could only get on its crest, then he was in with a chance.

Then, at just the right moment, Peter caught the wave and was up on his feet. Jack could hardly believe his eyes as the crest soared above Crab Rock with Peter balancing on Tom's board.

Brilliant! You've done it! You've surfed Crab Rock!

Peter was gliding towards the shore now, still on the wave, cheering and clapping. Then, for no reason, he fell off his board. To Jack, it looked as if someone had pushed him.

Jack swam towards Peter in a fast crawl, pushing himself harder than he had ever done before, but he knew he wasn't making enough progress.

As Peter struggled in the current, Jack saw him go under.

Hang on! I'm coming. Just hang on.

Although Peter bobbed up and swam a few more feeble strokes, he soon went under again.

Jack raced through the waves, his muscles screaming. When he looked up, Peter was even farther away.

Jack was trying to be brave, to sound more confident than he felt. Peter was being dragged further and further away. He'd drown if Jack didn't reach him soon.

Suddenly, the waves around Jack turned golden and, although the crests hadn't broken, spray leapt into the air and began to make a human shape. It hung in the air just above the surface of the sea.

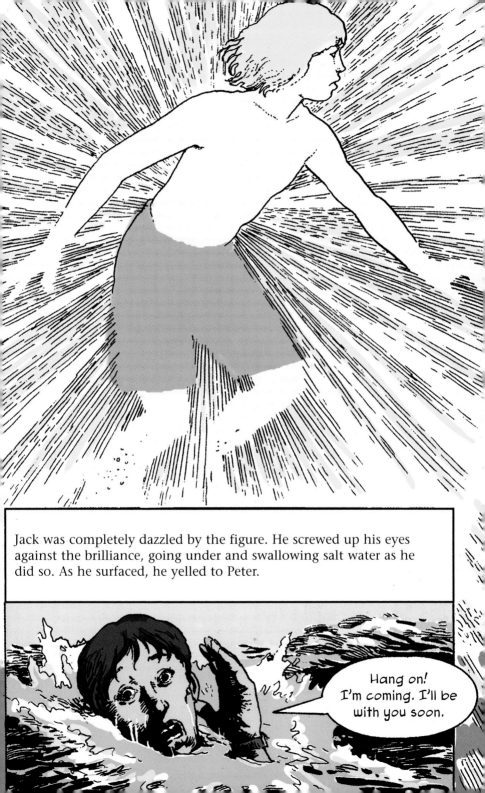

Jack was completely dazzled by the figure. He screwed up his eyes against the brilliance, going under and swallowing salt water as he did so. As he surfaced, he yelled to Peter.

Jack watched as the sparkling figure with the blond hair stood up on the old board and headed towards Peter. Peter was still struggling, each stroke weaker than the last.

Then Tom bent down and with easy strength pulled Peter up on to the old board.

I surfed Crab Rock. Did you see me, Tom? You're free now. Free to go.

Watching intently, Jack saw Tom move slightly to the rear of the board, his ghostly body shimmering in the golden surf.

Then the brothers caught a wave that gently took them into shallow water.

Suddenly another wave broke and Jack was carried towards the beach in a sheet of spray. As he headed towards the shore, Tom's sparkling figure passed him, going the other way, without the board.

His feet were balanced on a wave that was running in the wrong direction, sending him hurtling toward the horizon.

Jack found Peter standing in the shallows, clutching the old, battered board.

He'll be all right now.

Yes, I think he will.

He'd want you to have this.

I can't. You surfed Crab Rock, not me.